T0385124

TELLING STORIES

TELLING STORIES
PHOTOGRAPHS OF THE FALL

KEVIN CUMMINS

FOREWORD BY SIMON ARMITAGE

MITCHELL BEAZLEY

"First of all you want to tell a story, but images are what are going to shore it up and get to the heart of the matter."

ANNE SEXTON

The Fall are an ugly band. It's part of the attraction. They make a noise that to many people borders on the offensive. When US Forces laid siege to opera-loving Panamanian dictator General Noriega in Panama City's Vatican Embassy, they surrounded the building with loudspeakers and eventually "smoked" him out with a playlist that included songs from pop and rock's jukebox of sonic horror. Noriega stuck it out for about two weeks, but I always thought that a quick barrage of *Hex Enduction Hour* or *Room To Live* would have brought a speedier conclusion, the surrendering military leader emerging with his hands over his ears, screaming, "Enough, enough."

I say this as someone who has witnessed the curdled faces and curled toes of listeners who have experienced The Fall either accidentally or at my insistence, people who heard only discord and incompetence when the likes of "Noel's Chemical Effluence" or "Spoilt Victorian Child" were aimed in their direction. But my ears are different. In my ears, then in my brain, The Fall produce a sound which appeals to some fundamental part of my social and psychological identity, and speaks directly to my understanding of what music can be. I find them urgent, powerful, exciting, mesmerizing. Unlike some, I DO NOT LISTEN TO THE FALL FOR REASONS OF IRONY or out of INTELLECTUAL CURIOSITY – I actually LIKE THEM. And if I say they *disturb* me, I mean that they provoke a response – cerebral, linguistic, emotional, cultural, political – like no other work of art, be it a film, a painting or (I admit it) a poem. They also incite a physical reaction, something I feel materially, in my neck, wrists and at other pulse points around my body. The Fall aren't known for their floor-fillers but I have a playlist lined up and ready to roll, a selection of infectiously danceable choons, from the heavy stomp of "Mountain Energei", to the jaunty pop jig of "Victoria", to the trippy trance beat

of "Powderkex", to the madcap psychobilly of "Tommy Shooter", to the fuzzy mosh pit thrash of "Container Drivers". Fall Disco DJ: call me; available.

Being a Fall fan can be an unglamorous occupation. It's partly an age thing. If you were 16 or 17 the year *Live at the Witch Trials* or *Dragnet* came out, you're now in your late 50s, the age your mum and dad were when everything they said about "popular music" was the killjoy spiel of out-of-touch fuddy duddies. Telling someone you're going upstairs to listen to The Fall (as an activity it's often undertaken privately, in distant rooms or on well-insulated headphones) is like saying you're going back to your taxidermy project. On the other hand, it's a badge of honour within the higher regions of musical discourse. There's something unanswerable about wearing a Fall T-shirt or recommending an album or quoting a line, a kind of trump card in the rock-and-roll-conversation game. There's something comforting, too, about finding other Fall fans, confirming that you're not alone in the universe and that your taste in music is, in fact, discerning rather than defective or plain old broke. And, of course, The Fall are now *eternal*: most music fails to outlive the era of its emergence, but The Fall sound has matured with age. The day I was approached to write this foreword I'd been listening to *Your Future Our Clutter* on vinyl for about six hours solid. Just kept changing the discs or flipping them over (vinyl, double album) then dropping the needle on the outer circumference again, and could have happily gone on doing it into the night. You can't write for posterity – it's a mug's game because we've no idea what the future will be like – but The Fall never belonged to a specific musical period or style, so have remained timeless. (It's one of the reasons why I continue to write about them in the present tense, even though they no longer exist.) A lack of commercial success and general unpopularity among the

masses probably helped; they could never sell out because they had nothing shallow or worthless to flog.

It's both a fallacy and a disservice to other band members to say that Mark E Smith is The Fall and The Fall is Smith. Yet it's hardly a surprise that the spotlight always fell on him once his personality and the band's *modus operandi* became indistinguishable. As his reputation for idiosyncrasy grew, convention dictated that all encounters with M E S should be recorded as evidence of eccentricity and elevated to the status of folklore. The punch-up with (or maybe just getting punched *by*) Marc Riley, for example. Or his antics at the ICA prior to and during his interview with Michael Bracewell. And the story about him inviting music journalist David Cavanagh back to his flat to cook him a meal, then emerging from the kitchen half an hour later with a crisp sandwich. When the artist Anthony Frost described Smith's wake to me, it sounded like one of those big set-piece scenes from *Shameless*. Frost was a trusted friend of Smith's and a frequent collaborator (posters, album and single covers, stage backdrops, T-shirts). An unlikely alliance, you might think, given Frost's unapologetically abstract aesthetic and Smith's penchant for the kitchen-sink realism of everyday life. Many of Frost's works have the names of The Fall tracks as their titles. His painting *Blue Rush* for the cover of *Imperial Wax Solvent* once hung in a St Ives restaurant but now hangs in my house, though the right way up, not sideways on as it appeared on the album. Conforming to those anecdotal expectations, my own brief meetings with Smith have, over time, lapsed into cartoons or sketches. In the Netherlands, at a music and poetry festival, I made the neophyte's mistake of approaching him and telling him what a big fan I was. "Never mind that, cock, get me a light for this fag." At Réification, the 24-hour Tony Wilson shindig in a marquee (cha! cha!) near Victoria Station in summer 2008, whatever he was saying to me came out largely as pungent smoke rings, or was drowned by the raucous banter of other Manchester music veterans and ex-Factory workers. Plus, I had half an ear turned to the stage where A Certain Ratio were playing their ethereal punk-funk for the first time in an age. And in the "green room" at Huddersfield University he cut an aloof figure, prowling the corridor between offices, scrutinizing memos and defacing bulletins pinned to a noticeboard, eventually sloping off to an empty classroom and shutting the door behind him. That was October 2005 by my reckoning; the gig was a good one, a bonus really, because going to see The Fall was only occasionally about the music itself. More of a booster dose of anti-establishmentism and a vote for ugliness, or at least that's how I justified buying tickets for show after show after show, some of which were pretty shambolic. A few years later I saw them at Holmfirth Picturedrome. The recollection may have morphed into a weird dream and no doubt someone on a Fall forum will correct me if I'm wrong, but in my memory Smith left the stage quite early in the performance, taking the mic with him on a very long cable. Knowing the internal geography of the backstage area of that venue as I do, I'm pretty confident he "sang" for the rest of the show in the toilet, and quite possibly on it.

No one has captured the look of alternative UK music over the past half a century more tellingly than Kevin Cummins. And even though his camera has swung in many directions, there's a kind of Mancunian dialect to his art, a sort of default focal length or fixed stare that always returns to the shadows and reflections of his hometown. Peer into the pit of his eye and I suspect you'd see the silhouettes of Ian Curtis, Ian Brown, Howard Devoto, the Gallaghers, Pete Shelley, Shaun Ryder, Morrissey et al, set against a backdrop of Heaton Park or the Arndale.

From those 1976 Sex Pistols gigs at the Lesser Free Trade Hall (called "legendary" so often they have passed into fiction) to wherever we are now, via everything that happened in between, Cummins has borne witness. Until Mark E Smith's death in early 2018, The Fall were a constant presence in that timeline, and seeing these photographs in one book, start to finish, brings a visual narrative to a history I have only ever considered in audio terms. If this collection is the photographic equivalent of a Fall discography, it's also a publication that questions the received wisdom about the *appearance* of The Fall, a wisdom I've casually accepted over the years, based on the slapdash iconography, scrapbook imagery and scrawled sleeve notes of their record covers or gig posters. Viewed in that light, The Fall were always anti-fashion, with Smith himself taking it to another level. Seen through that lens, he didn't so much wear clothes as sabotage them. Anything he donned looked instantly second-hand. His vibe, whether achieved or involuntary, was that of a released prisoner passing through the gates of Strangeways wearing the same clothes he'd handed in a couple of decades earlier, now ill-fitting and perfectly out of date but still reeking of Capstan Full Strength. Even in the Brix era, when either Mrs Smith or an over-enthusiastic/misguided record-label marketing manager had frogmarched him down to Topshop or Afflecks Palace, shirts still hung skew-whiff from the buckled coat hanger of his shoulders, and his kecks looked borrowed. And his shoes were the only things left in the spare bedroom after a house clearance etc, etc. The same kind of contextual logic was applied to Smith's face, a façade slowly imploding under the force of gravity and being eaten away from the inside by booze, speed and a sort of flesh-eating cynicism, as if his cheekbones were finally succumbing to the relentless assault of his abrasive opinions. Cummins doesn't exactly make The Fall catwalk contenders or present a revisionist visual history of the band that repositions them as misunderstood fashionistas of their day. But I find in his photographs a true respect for their art and a genuine understanding of their attitudes, arrived at through perspectives and camera angles that rescue the band from caricature and cliché. To photograph The Fall *completely* would require a very wide wide-angle lens, given the well-catalogued cabinet reshuffles over the years, some of which were entire regime changes. Presented chronologically, this collection of images gets beyond the pantomime politics and delivers something more domestic in tone – like a family album, subconsciously documenting all the passion, complexity and dysfunction of the typical family unit, including marriages, divorces, adoptions, feuds, flounce-outs, affairs, sibling rivalries, births, bereavements, celebrations, anniversaries and all the usual Freudian intrigue. It's a work of generational progress that follows Smith from boyish teenager to the godfather of a large and splintered dynasty. In some of the final portraits, new band members stand around him like grandchildren. Either that, or Cummins has created a sense of The Fall as a living being or physical entity, a shapeshifting, skin-shedding manifestation, with its one permanent member as the most recognizable body part. In some of the earlier, innocent photographs, the ugliest band in the world looks almost beautiful.

The Fall are a phenomenon, and one with very few parallels given the unbroken longevity of the project, the astonishing productivity, and the way the band maintained its cult status from start to finish. Most bands fail, and those that succeed often do so by becoming fools or their own tribute acts. The Fall never conquered the planet or even the charts, but they survived, and did so by composing suicide notes to the music industry, album after album after album. And every resurrection was a revelation.

INTRODUCTION
KEVIN CUMMINS

"The way to begin a story depends not so much upon what you mean by a story as upon the story itself and the public for which it is intended."

DYLAN THOMAS

The way to begin a story about The Fall is a challenge. This is mainly because there was something of a swirling chaos about the band – unexplained changes, absences, conflict, a vortex of disarray, with one solid lynchpin holding things together at the centre: Mark E Smith. My story of The Fall is a long but fragmented one. I began photographing them at the beginning of their career in 1977 and continued to drop in and out of their story over the next 40 years. On and off during that time, I tried in my photographs to still that chaos, to capture moments of The Fall and pin them, almost anaesthetize them, into a frame of stillness – a word that is not often associated with the band.

My initial encounter with them was far from still. My first feature had just been published in *NME* at the end of July 1977, when I was commissioned to shoot The Fall in concert a few weeks later in August. This was a live show at a youth club in Collyhurst, a suburb of Manchester. It was obvious that the venue was totally inappropriate. The 50p tickets had hastily been reduced to 20p but there still weren't many takers, even at that rock-bottom price. After three songs, the guy who ran the place came on stage and told Mark that it was too loud for their young audience and that the songs weren't "quite right" for them either. He then suggested that they leave. I'm not sure if he ever returned everyone's 20 pence, because the band's manager made a quick phone call to The Ranch Bar on Dale Street in central Manchester, a mile away, where they were delighted to accommodate them at short notice, and the rest of the gig was played out there.

One of the first live portraits I took of Mark opens this book. It was taken in St George's Community Centre in the youth club, just before the band were "removed" to The Ranch. Mark looks impossibly young, wearing his Rock Against Racism badge, holding onto the mic stand and staring thoughtfully at the ground. We were both young then and my story of The Fall is one of us maturing together in our respective careers. In those early days, I gave the band, and especially Mark, much more autonomy in how I photographed them. But as I became familiar with him and realized that he did not care how he – or the band in general – were represented visually, this opened up and changed how I photographed him.

If you study the photographs, you will see that Mark's face dominates the space, even if he's only in 20 per cent of the frame. Looking back, it seems in many ways as though my visual representations accurately reflected what was going on in the band – I was centring the chaos, pinning down the one immovable part. Being given a blank slate to work with also allowed me to be more experimental than I might otherwise have been. As I grew in confidence as a photographer, this became more evident in some of the single portraits, especially the later ones. There is a rawness about them, an unflinching lens capturing Mark's physical changes. I knew when I photographed him that I did not have to dress up any of the images in any way. This is most obvious in some of the last shots I took in March 2011, when Mark resembled something of a figure in a Francis Bacon painting. Dressed in a black jumper and leather jacket, he appears contorted, leaning and gurning toward the camera, mouth drooping, sores at the corner of his lips, hair long and dishevelled. I took these photographs against the wall of a car park in Salford. Urban, but dripping with old paint like a disused canvas. Oddly, that car park is still there, the wall is still there, grass shooting through the concrete, razor wire to the left. There is something poignant about the persistence of that place, remaining there a decade later, greening grass shoots every year in contrast to Mark's now permanent absence.

Even though I love those last portraits, the final few years of Mark's life were tough. I found it difficult to watch his physical decline, so I turned down a couple of commissions to photograph him. I felt it unlikely that I could better that session in Salford from March 2011. I took a few pictures at a gig at The Garage in Islington in 2014, and the shot on page 247 became my final photo of Mark. I love his youthful insouciance in that photograph. It says so much about him. He was in a spirited mood that night, playing with the audience. I stood at the side of the stage with my camera fixed in position, as you do with live shots, waiting and hoping something would happen. Then it did. Mark is captured like an animated showman, hand thrown wide, almost as if he is frozen mid-anecdote, telling a story.

And photographs tell unique stories. The collection of images in this book document their own visual stories in as chronological a way as possible when you are trying to pin down something that rarely stays still. Many of the sessions are accompanied by my memories of the shoot, a glimpse behind the scenes, telling stories about and on The Fall. I do not think that Mark would mind this. He had a playful side. Often, after we arranged to meet for a band shoot, it would only be Mark who would turn up. Usually late. Generally, in a completely different place to the one we'd arranged. Invariably that would be a pub. He was demanding and desperately curmudgeonly at times. Before we started, he would want to have a drink and a catch-up, then tell me he hadn't got time for photos and could we do them another day. He once played the

best part of a Haçienda gig with his back to the audience, because he thought it would make it difficult for me to take a photo to accompany the *NME* review. Yet none of this behaviour bothered me. Probably because in so many other ways I found him to be great – often challenging – company, but he was always keen to discuss current affairs, music, literature and football, especially the woes of supporting Manchester City. Not in a bombastic blokey way either. He was always open to new ideas. He would argue exhaustively about something he firmly believed in, but he would listen too.

And it is this combination of creative, thoughtful listener that often makes the best photographic study. There is much to try and capture, a depth. There is nothing docile about my images of The Fall. Despite a diverse line-up, despite absences and changes of appearance, there is always a vitality, an immutable essence. They delight, they disturb, they reveal the passing of time, and I suppose, ultimately, they show loss. Yet they also restore that loss. Because, just for one moment, you can look at these images and remember. Mark is back with us wearing his unwieldy shirts with his disgruntled face. He is on stage again. He is smoking. He is standing in the snow by iron railings. Time does not matter. He will always be there in these images, unmoving, the essential centre of chaos.

ST. GEORGES' COMMUNITY CENTRE

Livesey Street, Manchester

DISCO

plus Live Group - "THE FALL"

on Thursday, 18th August, 1977

7-30 p.m. until 10-30 p.m.

Admission 50 pence

ST GEORGE'S HALL,
COLLYHURST, MANCHESTER
18 AUGUST 1977

THE RANCH BAR
DALE STREET, MANCHESTER
18 AUGUST 1977

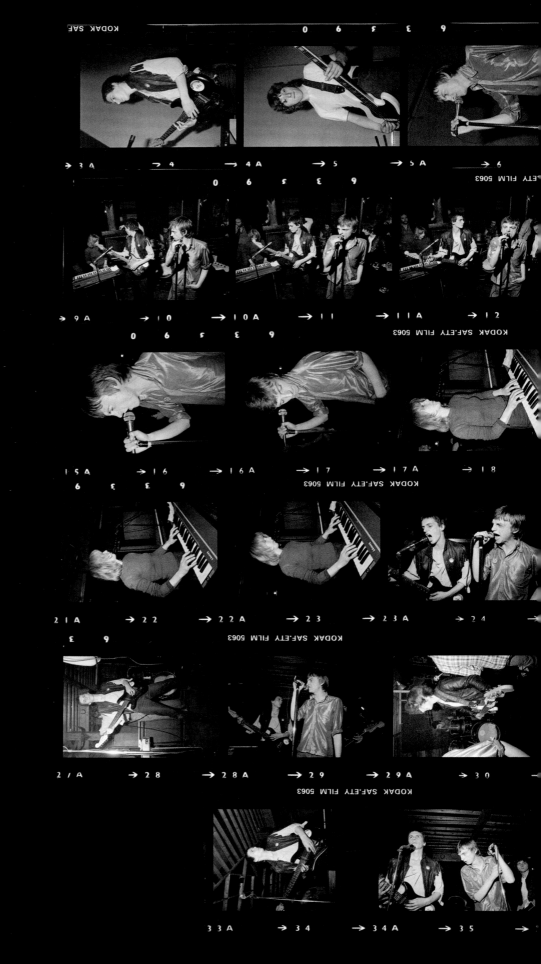

KODAK SAFETY FILM
KODAK SAFETY FILM 5063

→ 7 → 7 A → 8 → 8 A → 9

KODAK SAFETY FILM 5063

→ 13 → 13 A → 14 → 14 A → 15

KODAK SAFETY FILM 5063

→ 19 → 19 A → 20 → 20 A → 21

KODAK SAFETY FILM 5063

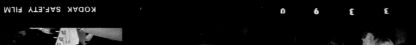

→ 25 → 25 A → 26 → 26 A → 27

KODAK SAFETY FILM

→ 31 → 31 A → 32 → 32 A → 33

KODAK SAFETY FILM 5063

→ 36 → 36 A → 37 → 37 A → 38

THE ELECTRIC CIRCUS
COLLYHURST, MANCHESTER
2 OCTOBER 1977

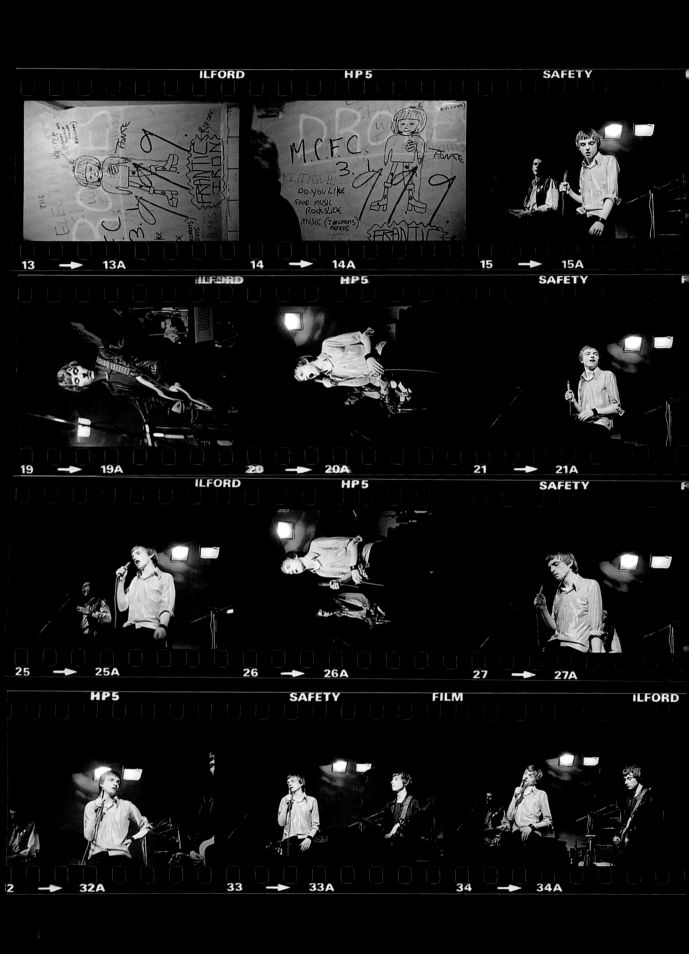

MARK'S FLAT
PRESTWICH
21 DECEMBER 1977

Mark decided that he wanted me to photograph him and
the band at his flat in Prestwich. Neither he nor I wanted
to do the typical rock 'n' roll band shots, and so he thought
it'd be amusing to do the kind of "at home" feature that
was popular in the Manchester City match programme
back then.

   Mark was a big City fan, and so am I. It was a very
un-rock 'n' roll idea, which suited me. But there was also
a world of difference between a shot of City "hero"
Dennis Tueart in a leafy Cheshire mansion and The Fall
in a post-student flat in Prestwich. But maybe that was
the point of it.

   The room was claustrophobically small, with political
posters and flyers for gigs taped to the walls. The concept
of washing cups and dishes clearly hadn't occurred to
Mark. There was also quite a lot of detritus on the floor,
which he helpfully pushed under the sofa, and then said,
"Right cocker, can we get on with this. I'm going to need a
pint soon."

   I was slightly worried that a "domestic bliss" shot
wouldn't be what the *NME* wanted, so I finished the
session outside Prestwich Hospital. We then repaired to
a nearby pub. Until I processed the film, I hadn't noticed
that Mark was holding his cat. That outdoor shot –
naturally – was the one the *NME* used.

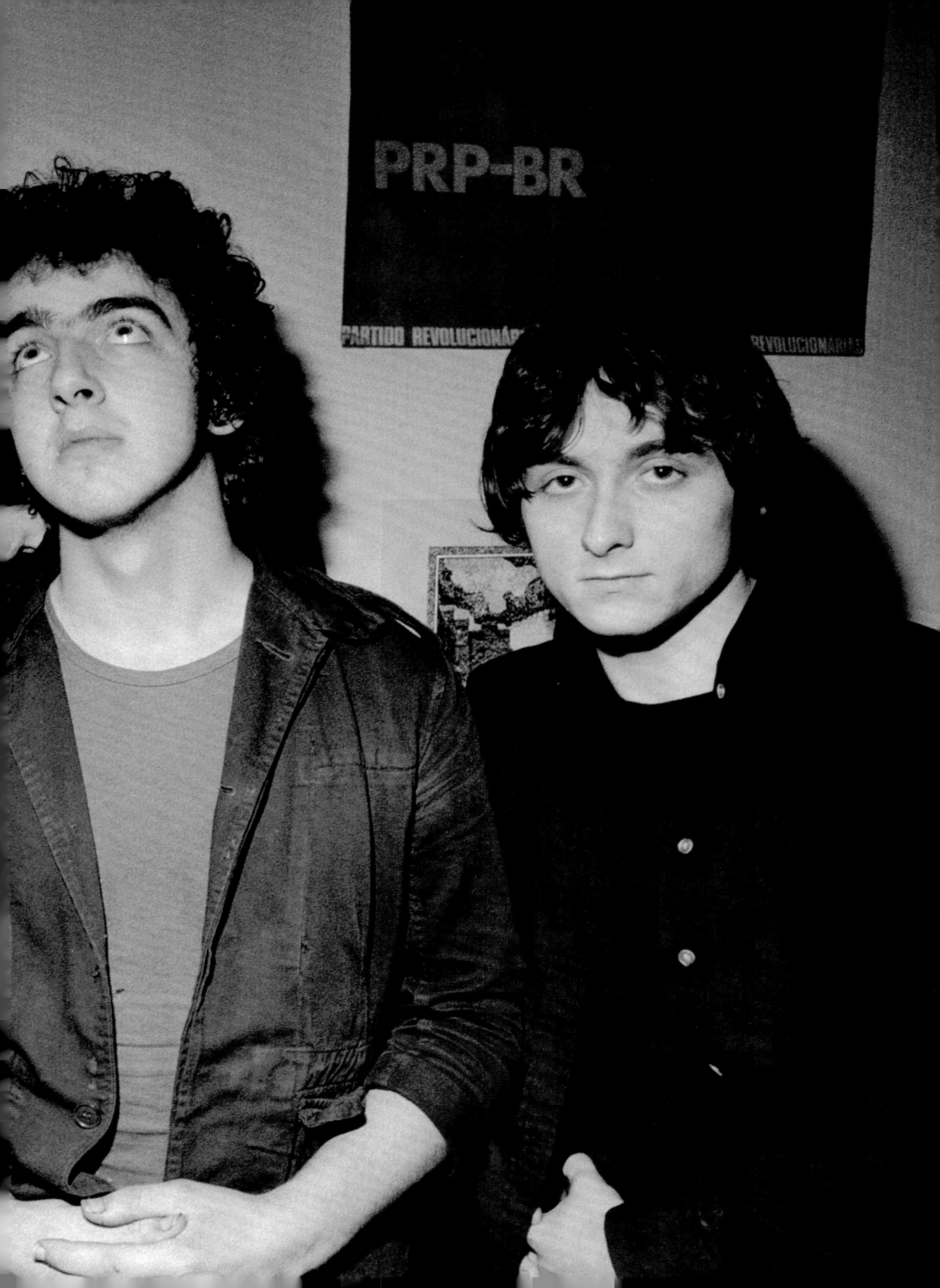

Kingswood Clinic

T J DAVIDSON'S REHEARSAL ROOMS
LITTLE PETER STREET, MANCHESTER
APRIL 1978

MANCHESTER CITY CENTRE
APRIL 1978

THE RELIGIOUS SOCI

"The most u
truth is a sa
than the pl
falsehood

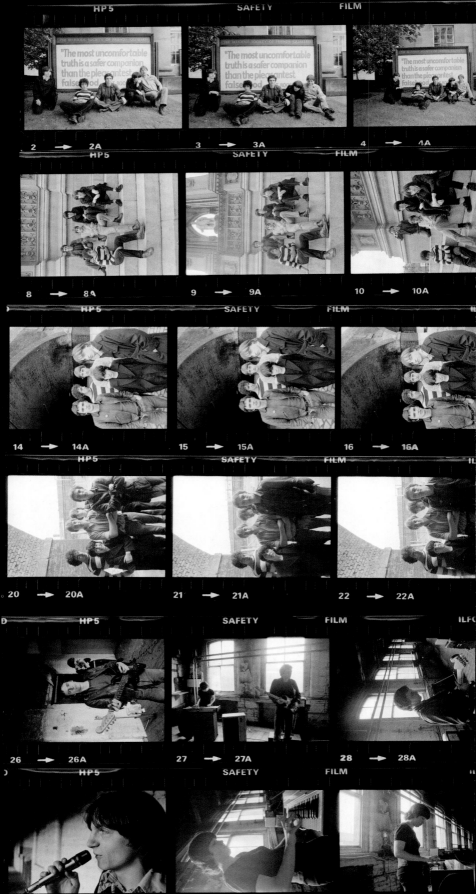

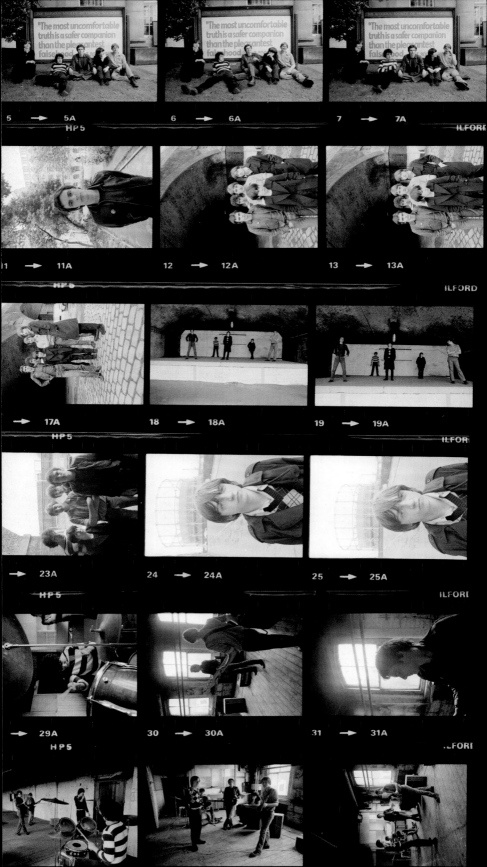

STUFF THE SUPERSTARS SPECIAL
THE MAYFLOWER
BIRCH STREET, GORTON, MANCHESTER
28 JULY 1979

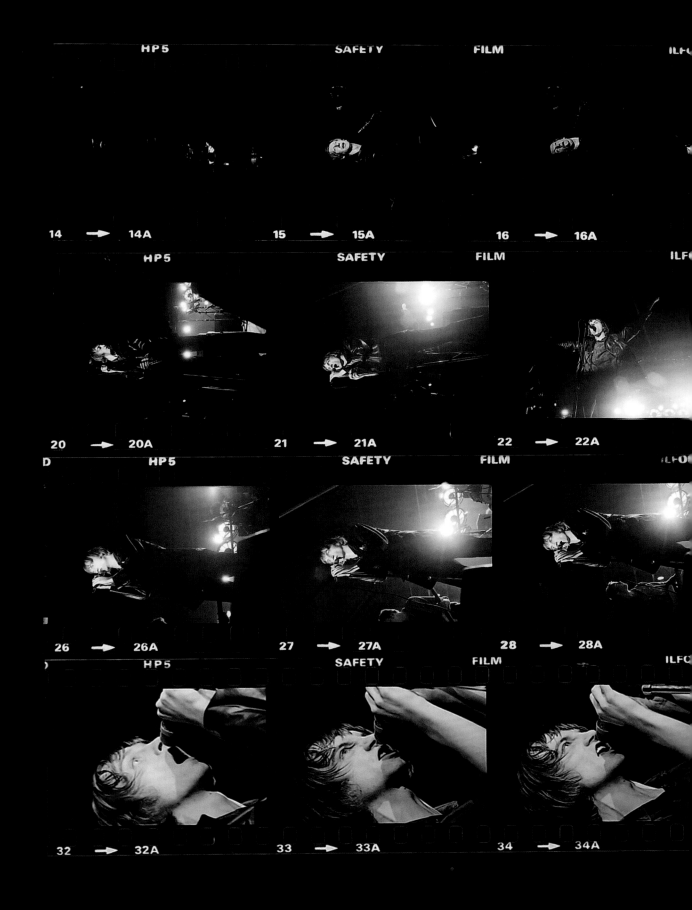

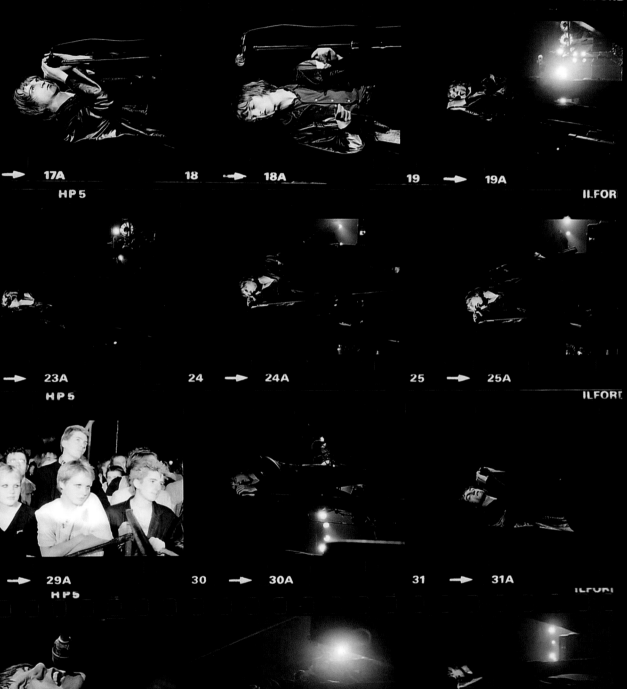

RAFTERS
OXFORD ROAD, MANCHESTER
31 JULY 1980

ILFORD

6 → 6A   7 → 7A   8 → 8

ILFORD

12 → 12A   13 → 13A   14 →

ILFORD

18 → 18A   19 → 19A   20 →

ILFORD

24 → 24A   25 → 25A   26 →

ILFORD   HP

30 → 30A   31 → 31A   32 → 32A

ILFORD

36 → 36A   37 → 37A   38 → 38A

PRESTWICH CLOUGH
16 JANUARY 1981

FESTIVAL OF THE TENTH SUMMER
G-MEX CENTRE, MANCHESTER
19 JULY 1986

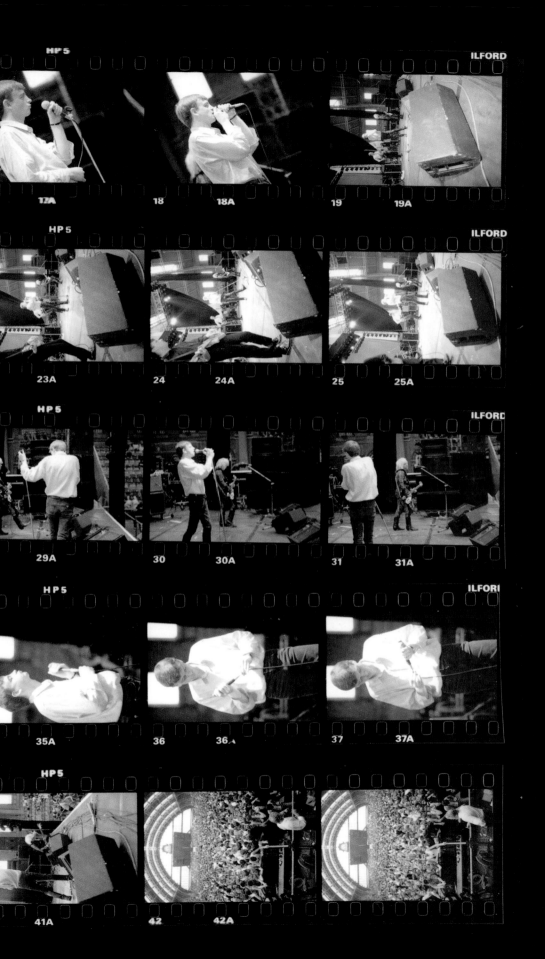

I AM CURIOUS, ORANGE
KING'S THEATRE, EDINBURGH
19 AUGUST 1988

In August 1988, I shot the photos for *I Am Curious, Orange*
for an *NME* cover. I flew to Edinburgh overnight from
San Francisco, where I had been shooting The Sugarcubes,
as I was genuinely excited about photographing The
Fall doing something that sounded so experimentally
different. I also didn't want to miss seeing the show at
the Edinburgh Festival. The job hadn't been confirmed
when I was due to leave California, but I decided to go
anyway. Nobody met me when I landed at Edinburgh,
and it was too early for anyone in a band to be awake. A big
drawback was that not only did I not know where anyone
was staying, I still had no idea what time the shoot would
be or if it was happening at all. Finally, I saw an ad for the
show, which at least gave me some indication of where
they would be. After standing outside the King's Theatre
for a couple of hours, the band eventually turned up and
Mark said, "You found us then, you'd better come in." An
hour or so later, they ran through a couple of numbers then
wheeled the giant burger on stage for the main photos.
Once the set had been dismantled and I was packing my
equipment away, Mark said, "Can we have some of those
for the album cover?" I asked him why he hadn't said
something earlier, as I could have taken some variations,
to which he replied, "You'd have wanted to charge us. This
way we can just have an *NME* photo or two. They pay you
enough, don't they?"

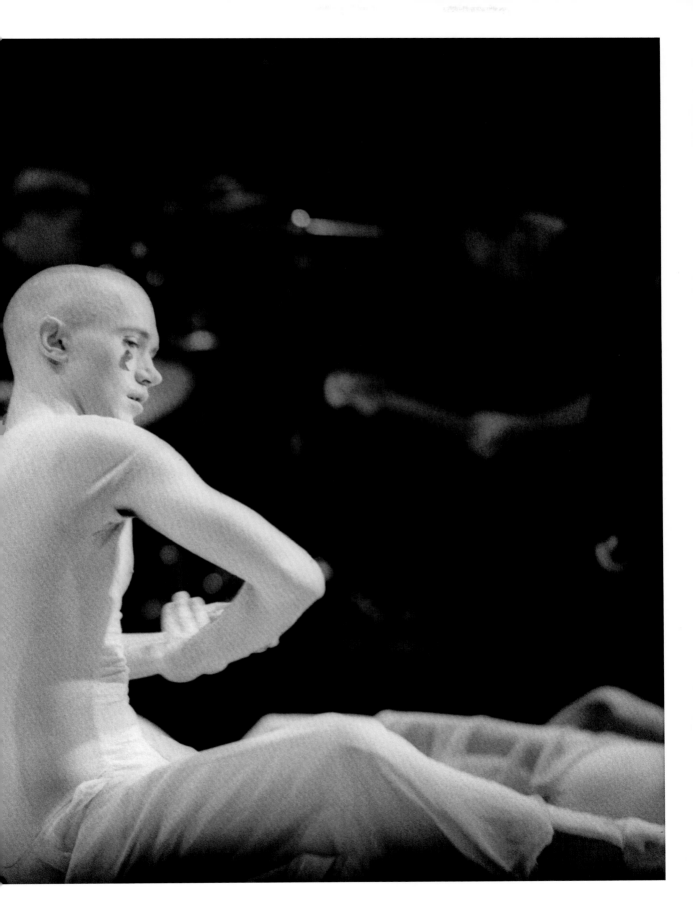

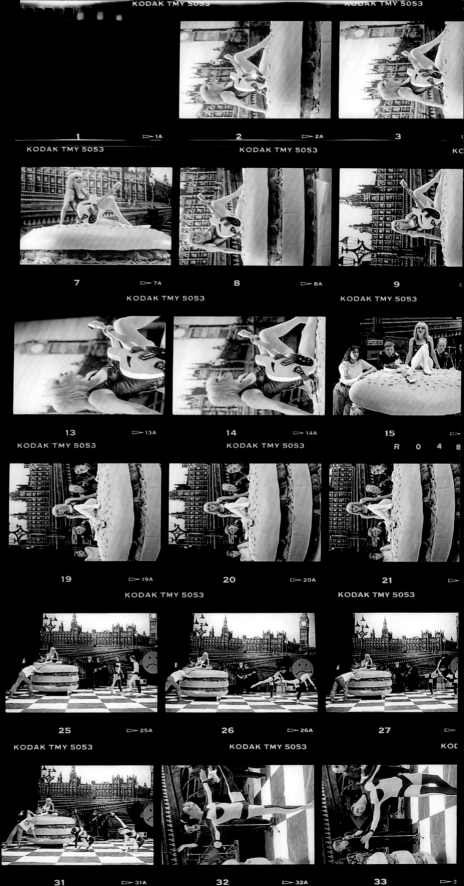

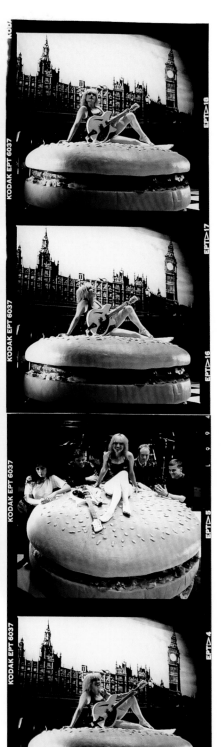

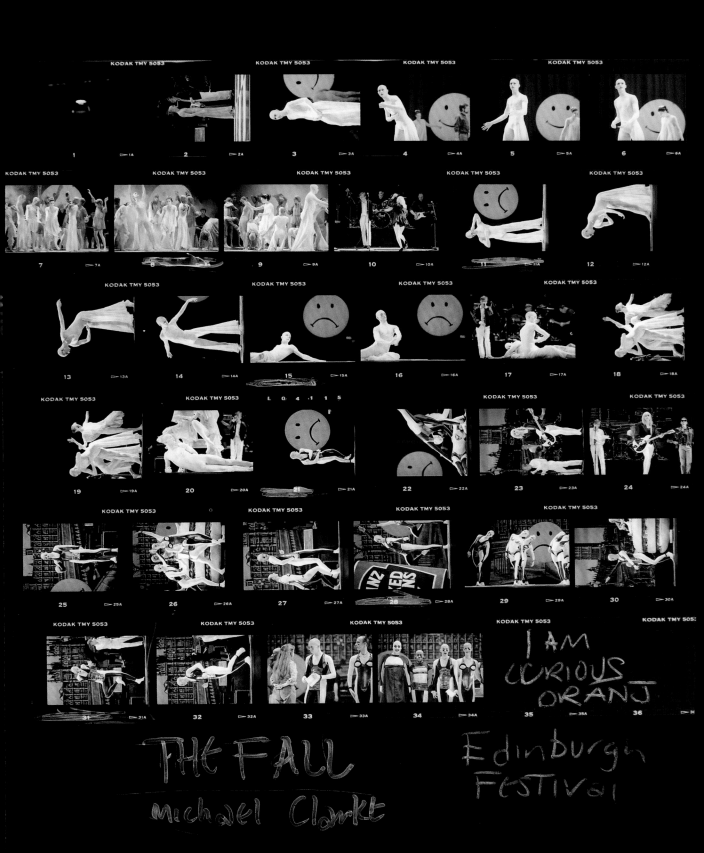

THE HAÇIENDA
MANCHESTER
18 DECEMBER 1989

LONDON
2 AUGUST 1992

LONDON
10 MARCH 1993

MY

31
35

KODAK 5053 TMY

31A

32
36

KODAK 5053 TMY

32A

33

33A

34

34A

35

35A

36

36A

KC 10 0393A

GREENGATE
SALFORD
22 AUGUST 2005

In 2005, I went to photograph The Fall for their label, Sanctuary. Everyone assumed it'd run smoothly because I knew Mark, so they didn't send a PR with me. I went to the rehearsal room at the appointed time, but it was locked up. I assumed he (and the band) would be in the nearest pub. They were.

"You took your time, Cocker," said Mark.

The pub was in a pretty dodgy part of Salford. All the curtains were closed, as if they hadn't been told about the years-old change in the licensing laws allowing them to open in the afternoon. I took my camera out to get a photo of Mark with a pint – to add to my collection of similar shots – when a fearsome-looking guy who had been drinking in the vault came in and asked why I was taking Mark's photo.

Mark said, "He fancies me."

The guy ignored it, looked around and saw guitar cases. He asked if we were a band. Mark ignored him. He asked again and added, "Would I have heard of you?"

Mark stared him down and replied, "How the fuck do I know what you've heard of?"

"Try me," said the guy, with a mix of menace and worn-down patience.

Mark took a mouthful of beer, stared at him, and said, "The Fucking Beatles".

The rest of the band held their breath and stared into their pints.

The guy looked down at Mark, who had continued to concentrate on his pint, and said, "Good name, mate." Then turned and walked back into the other room.

Nobody spoke until Mark said, "Are we having another one then?" He looked at me and continued, "It's got to be Salford's richest man's round."

260805-3

KODAK 400TMY   53

KODAK 400TMY   52

400TMY

ILFORD HP5 PLUS

1 2 3

5 1 7 1

ILFORD HP5 PLUS

7 7A 8 8A 9 9

ILFORD HP5 PLUS 5 1 7 1 ILFORD HP5 PLUS

13 13A 14 14A 15 15

PLUS ILFORD HP5 PLUS 5 1 7 1

19 19A 20 20A 21 2

7 1 ILFORD HP5 PLUS ILFORD HP5 PLI

25 25A 26 26A 27 2

RD HP5 PLUS 5 1 7 1 ILFORD HP5 PLUS

31 31A 32 32A 33

ILFORD HP5 PLUS

HP5 PLUS   5   1   7   1   ILFORD HP5 PLUS

ILFORD HP5 PLUS   5   1   7   1   ILFORD HP5

ILFORD HP5 PLUS   ILFORD HP5 PLUS   5   1

5   1   7   1   ILFORD HP5 PLUS   ILF

ILFORD HP5 PLUS   5   1   7   1   ILFORD HP5 PLUS

26080S-1

BERLIN AND
MARIA AM OSTBAHNHOF, BERLIN
21 APRIL 2006

In 2006, I went to Berlin with the band to take some more photos for their label. Before the gig, I met up with a glum-looking Steve Trafford, then the current guitarist, outside a bar. He told me he wouldn't be surprised if the gig didn't happen that evening. Apparently, Mark had been furious that he couldn't smoke en route at Frankfurt Airport. Then, when they'd arrived in Berlin and got a cab, Mark lit up. The driver told him he couldn't smoke in his cab. Mark told him he'd smoke wherever he wanted to. When the cab stopped at a red light, the driver turned round and snatched the cigarette out of Mark's mouth. Mark punched him. The driver punched him back. Unbeknown to everyone in the vehicle, a local TV crew just happened to be filming a news item at that junction. When they heard the commotion in the cab next to them, they turned the cameras on and filmed this impromptu news story playing out in front of them. When it finally calmed down, they told the cab driver that they had enough "evidence" if he wanted to pursue it further. The tour manager then sorted it out in the way tour managers with a pocket full of cash often do.

Mark was still incandescent with rage. When he finally got in his hotel room, he took his dentures out and banged them down on his bedside table. They bounced off onto the floor, and while stomping around the room looking for them, he stood on them. Eleni, Mark's then wife, was dispatched to the nearest "24-hour Emergency Denture Repair Shop" and the band went to the nearest pub. A few weeks later, when the tour reached the USA, the band couldn't take any more of his erratic behaviour. They were plotting to leave early without mentioning it to Mark. He obviously found out, confronted them during a soundcheck and sacked them all (but Eleni). Then he calmly asked his support band if they'd like to be "The Fall" for the rest of the tour.

HAMMERSMITH PALAIS
LONDON
1 APRIL 2007

This, my final session with Mark, was shot in Salford in March 2011. He was 58, but his health was deteriorating, and his skin was pretty poor too. He'd also lost a lot of weight.

I'd found a blue-grey painted wall, which looked almost canvas-like. I hoped to take a very traditional-style portrait against it. Mark couldn't stand still; he was throwing his head around and gurning for the camera. He looked like a character in a Francis Bacon painting. It was visceral and astonishing. I just kept taking photos until he wore himself out. Several frames from this session are among the most powerful portraits I've ever taken. They're also very difficult to view at times. But to me, they capture the spirit of Mark E Smith. Always challenging and pushing boundaries.

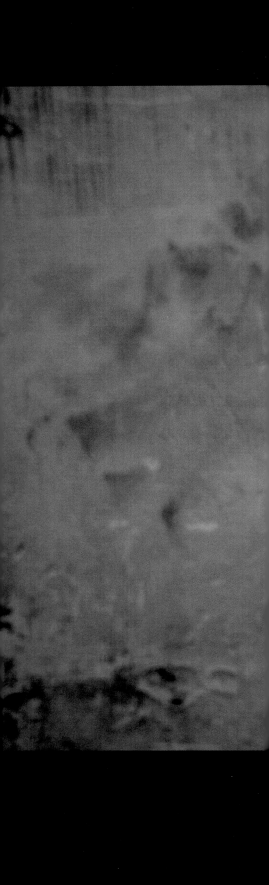

THE GARAGE
HOLLOWAY ROAD, ISLINGTON, LONDON
27 NOVEMBER 2014

This is the last photograph I took of Mark.

AFTERWORD
ELENI POULOU IN CONVERSATION, 2022

Kevin Cummins: What do you think Mark would have thought of a book of photographs about The Fall?
Eleni Poulou: Well, I think he would have preferred a book of photographs [to writing]. We had already started work on a coffee-table book of photographs of our tours in the States, but sadly we couldn't complete it. I think he would have felt that books about The Fall should be either photo books or in his own words. He wouldn't have really liked other people writing about him. You know, that was *his* job. The words.

Well, exactly. Absolutely.
And even visually he would have ideas. He was also a visual artist. He would maybe not take the photograph, but he would tell you what to do.

I think he always had very strong ideas of what he wanted to do. And, more often, what he didn't want to do, as well.
Definitely. A lot of his studying and research went not only into the good stuff – good literature and interesting art – but also the trivial. He called it "School TV", so we would watch a concert on TV to see what not to do.

When did you join The Fall and, more importantly, why did you join The Fall?
Mark and I met in 1995 and we hit it off famously, we were pen pals. But I had my own group back then – Zen-Faschisten – in fact, I was in several music groups, but Mark and I first went to the studio together and wrote in 1997. When I came to England to be with him, Mark was bankrupt, but had agreed to do a DVD that included playing some old songs – something he didn't like to do. They needed a keyboard player for that, so me and a girl called Ruth played for the DVD so we could fulfil the contract and pay the mortgage. Then the drummer from my group was living in New York, the singer was in Berlin

and I was in England, so it was near impossible for us to continue working together on a regular basis like we used to do. So, I had more time, and Mark asked me to join. I think I only wanted to do a bit of lyric writing, because we did the *Pander! Panda! Panzer!* spoken word album. We did that together, with samples that I had prepared, and lyrics. So at first I was writing lyrics mainly for him, and then I joined on keyboard.

Were you a fan of – were you a fan of The Fall before you joined them?
Yes. I mean, not a fan like idolizing them, you know. But I think, I still do think, there is no better band, so yes, of course I was. My cousin had played them to me when I was a child.

And what's your reaction to the fact that many fans see you as a saviour of The Fall? And how you added your weirdness to what was pretty much a fairly straight-ahead riff rock group at the time?
Well, that's very nice to hear. It was a heartfelt labour of love. Actually, I wouldn't even say a labour; we had become a team working together, and that means through the good and the bad times, in my book. And it wasn't always easy for Mark at that time. Like I said, he was bankrupt and we couldn't always get the shows he should have had. And so I tried to keep it in the spirit of The Fall, which always included women – though Mark didn't really differentiate – or which always had an element of outsiderness. Remember, he wanted to call it The Outsiders, as well, after the book. And in music you're always striving for the new sound, but you can't help but re-create something that was there before, or even borrow certain musical styles – a riff, a bassline, a melody – on purpose. But all in all, I think Mark always tried to do something that was avant-garde.

Definitely. But, to me, you changed their sound and it was by far the most inventive sound, in my opinion.

Thank you. I have to say, when you play it yourself many, many times on tour then it becomes more of a common thing. But at home we would do much weirder stuff: sound collages, sound poems and things like that, which never made it on record. So yes, I wish we would have done more of that.

Which period of The Fall do you think was the most progressively creative?

Oh Christ, to think about that! I think the beginning, because there was nothing like it at the time, or ever. I personally have a very soft spot for Nineties' The Fall, because I think, especially the lyrics, nobody had lyrics like that at the time. Maybe musically it was not so outlandish, but the lyrics were unreal. On *Middle Class Revolt* or records like that, I think that those lyrics should be set in stone and put up in front of libraries or something.

Brix called The Fall a "dictatorship" with Mark in control. Do you think that's accurate?

Obviously, it wasn't that at the beginning, when he was with Martin Braham as well. But a Fall album is a concept: it has a theme, it has a story, and it is one piece of art, like an exhibition. So he would shape that, but on the other hand he would let us be free in a way that I don't see any other bands being, unless you work in the realm of improvised music. If I came up with a riff, he'd say, "Great, let's try that"; if the guitarist had an idea, he'd be like, "Let's do that". He would always try it.

But when you were on stage, sometimes it was quite chaotic, when you were playing a live gig.

[laughs] Yeah.

I mean, did you know what Mark was going to do with your keyboard, for instance, and did you sometimes not even know what songs you were going to play?

No, we did have setlists, but...

You didn't always keep to it, though! I saw lots of setlists and half the songs were never played. He'd change his mind halfway through.

[laughs] You know what I particularly miss – he would also make up the lyrics halfway through to be topical. I would like to bring out CDs of the same Fall song – let's say, 35 versions of "Mountain Energei", live, of course, because every time they would have different lyrics. And not many bands do that. It's something. I think that part of being a writer and a poet is to comment on what's happening in the world right now, you know? And he did that famously.

It felt like "Mark versus technology" at times. How did you cope with that? Did you kind of find it amusing, or did it frustrate you?

I do miss it very much, being with somebody who's not constantly looking at his phone. He would constantly create something in the room, rearrange stuff, write stuff, draw comics instead.

I took a photograph at one gig of all the twisted mic leads and everything else. There was just this spaghetti mess of leads on the floor, halfway through the gig, and it was so obvious that it was a Fall gig. It couldn't have been anyone else.

[laughs] It was definitely a mass of cables and mic stands, and of course all the other debris that was left behind, like setlists and lyric sheets and all that. But sometimes I was really worried he would fall off stage, so I would play with

one eye watching that he didn't trip over a cable, and with the other hand I'd be texting the lighting guy to switch the strobe light off or something. You always had to have eyes on the back of your head!

We had songs like "Facebook Troll" [eventually called "Fibre Book Troll"], against technology, against social media. We would make fun of new phenomenon, like new dads or lad culture or whatever was around in the Nineties. But on the other hand, he was also embracing that new technology, so maybe during the Covid lockdowns, he would have had a blog or something. We don't know! It's possible. He needed time to write and to go to the pub, time alone to observe what other people do, in the pub or on the street.

Every day I try to find something new, even if it's mostly in the same cities or the same areas I still see some house I haven't seen before, or a shop or a weird sunset or something like that, to amuse. That is our own responsibility and Mark very much believed that you have to create your own life in an interesting way. You can't always wait for somebody to make it for you from the outside.

Did you sometimes find it quite difficult? Or was it easy to retain your autonomy while both living and working with Mark?
You sort of become very much part of *his* idea. So, I never thought about doing a solo thing, really, while I was with him. But I'm an only child, I'm also an island within myself and I'm a very permeable person.

And on a non-gig day, when you were at home, what was your daily routine as a couple?
At home we'd hang out together a lot and talk. Mark liked to talk. And I didn't drink at the time, but Mark would drink. So we would just hang out, talk, watch TV, listen

to music, dance... We danced a lot. I miss that so much. But we also talked about, like, bumping into strangers that would become friends. We'd go to the pub, and at the beginning we didn't even have our own TV, so we would go to the pub to watch TV together. We would go for walks and things like that. And we would also make music together, and listen to a lot of records.

I know that Mark read Arthur Machen and H P Lovecraft and I think they inspired his writing at times. But did he read much contemporary literature when you were together?
He did. He would also take recommendations or gifts from people, or would seek it out. If we travelled, we would go to bookshops. I always liked bringing home fanzines and graphic novels, and he liked them too. He read Michel Houellebecq and things like that. He would revisit things. I think that is a male thing – even young boys like to watch the same film again and again, whereas I like to see something new. He would also make something new out of something old, but in his special way. He would interweave thoughts and ideas and stories, like a collage, into something that was exciting. Even if it was based on something old, he would turn that around. And I like doing that too. But you have to be true to yourself, you have to describe what is happening in your vicinity and in your life. When I write a poem now, I don't think of something far, far away, I will include something that I saw with my own eyes yesterday.

Do you think there were lots of unfulfilled plans that Mark had? Do you think he would have written another play or a novel or anything?
Oh my god, yes. He would have done another record every year, hopefully more spoken word, because I think he really liked doing that, and maybe moved more into

narration and writing more screenplays. We were also planning to do something in a museum together. But you never know whether he might have picked up social media or not. Or he might have started playing an instrument. He wouldn't have wanted us to listen to the same old songs again and again. That's not what he wanted. He always wanted the next song.

Well, exactly. He'd criticize bands, maybe not publicly, but he'd criticize people for doing all these revival tours and just playing the same music over and over again, for going out playing their greatest hits and having the same setlist for the whole tour.
Exactly.

It's just not creative. What's the point?
But there is a comfort. If you are somewhere and you hear a song like a Northern Soul song or something that you have heard in your youth, and you feel something that you might have felt in your youth, you feel comfort. You might remember your mum singing it. That is all valid. We all have those comfort songs from the past. Mark had them too. But in your own work, especially with some of his contemporaries, there are bands that also started out in the Seventies as innovators and had a certain level of success, they will play what brings them the most money and standard. They will not suddenly start making very difficult string music or a complete U-turn to the sound their fans are used to.

Mark was always progressive and he would try something different, and that's why he would work with different bands and do quite surprising events. It was challenging for him in a way.
Yes, he also did some interesting collaborations. A lot of fans I meet are not white and not heterosexual or from

Europe. They are from all over the world, and some of them are 18! They never saw him live.

Tell me something that people don't know about Mark that would surprise them.
He was really good at taking a run-of-the-mill Hallmark or Post Office greetings card and turning it into the tiniest, loveliest thing you have ever seen. Honestly! Nobody else can do that.

ACKNOWLEDGEMENTS

Putting a book like this together is impossible without a good team around me, and once again I'm lucky to be working with the same core of people at Octopus who I've worked with now for several years.

My original editor, Joe Cottington, commissioned this book, but went elsewhere in the January transfer window. Fortunately, I was lucky enough to find a strong replacement in Alison Starling, whose help and support proved invaluable. Hopefully I wasn't too much trouble and maybe you'd like us to work together again.

Thanks also to Karen, Matt, Jonathan and Pauline for all helping to make this work – as ever. You're all great to deal with, even if my deadline surfing gives you all nightmares. Thanks also to Blake Lewis at Iconic for the scanning. His skills are second to none.

Massive thanks to my agent, Carrie Kania, whose constant support, and encouragement (and Champagne), kept me going through the tough winter months. The French House in Soho does a roaring trade every time I'm working on a new book. Long may it continue.

I couldn't have produced this book without Gail Crowther. Gail's ability to turn an average piece of prose into something of beauty is one of her many strengths. Gail sees things much more clearly than I do and has been invaluable in helping to give this book a true narrative flow, instead of it just plodding along. Gail is also more concise than I am and can strip back most of my multi-clause sentences into precise ten-word sentences that actually make sense. The book's title was Gail's idea – as was the Anne Sexton quote that opens the book. She also suggested telling stories to run alongside many of the sessions. Thanks a million, and the Champagne's on ice.

The stars are The Fall of course, and I must thank Eleni Poulou for her insight into life with Mark and for showing us his playful side, something many commentators have missed over the years. I'd also like to thank the former members of the band – too many to mention here by name of course – for all the years of listening pleasure they've given me.

I'd like to thank my friends in the MCFC "Arts Council" and my daughter Ella, and all the friends who I've been to Fall gigs with over the years, especially Steve Anglesey.

Also, thanks to Simon Armitage for writing the foreword. Simon is from the "wrong side" of the Pennines of course but is a huge fan of The Fall. I wasn't sure I was allowed to contact the Poet Laureate directly; I thought I might have to write to him via Her Majesty the Queen or with a case of Port attached to a hand-written note, but I emailed him anyway, and got an instant reply saying:

Hi Kevin,
Well, you've hit me in the soft spot here. Been listening to them all day actually, "Your Future Our Clutter". I can't explain it but every time I put one of their albums on, it sounds better. Their clutter, my future (I might use that).
Do you want me to write about the band, the music, or specifically the photos? I don't think I've ever really considered them as a visual entity, so that might be interesting. And I guess it would end up being sort of personal, because....it is.

So, thanks Simon. The Boys in Blue Never Give In.

Finally, thanks to Mark Edward Smith for the 40-year trip. I've missed your intoxicating conversation these past few years.

We all have stories to tell about our meetings with Mark. These are mine.

First published in Great Britain in 2022 by
Mitchell Beazley, an imprint of
Octopus Publishing Group Ltd
Carmelite House
50 Victoria Embankment
London EC4Y 0DZ
www.octopusbooks.co.uk

An Hachette UK Company
www.hachette.co.uk

Text and photographs copyright © Kevin Cummins 2022
Foreword text copyright © Simon Armitage 2022
Design and layout copyright © Octopus Publishing
Group 2022

Anne Sexton quotation on page 5 reprinted by permission
of SLL/Sterling Lord Literistic, Inc. Copyright by Linda
Gray Sexton and Loring Conant, Jr. 1981

Distributed in the US by
Hachette Book Group
1290 Avenue of the Americas
4th and 5th Floors
New York, NY 10104

Distributed in Canada by
Canadian Manda Group
664 Annette Street
Toronto, Ontario, Canada M6S 2C8

All rights reserved. No part of this work may be
reproduced or utilized in any form or by any means,
electronic or mechanical, including photocopying,
recording or by any information storage and retrieval
system, without the prior written permission of
the publisher.

The right of Kevin Cummins to be identified as the author
of this Work has been asserted by him in accordance with
the Copyright, Designs & Patents Act 1988

ISBN 978-1-78472-825-0

A CIP catalogue record for this book is available from the
British Library.

Printed and bound in China

10 9 8 7 6 5 4 3 2 1

Publisher: Alison Starling
Senior Editor: Pauline Bache
Creative Director: Jonathan Christie
Senior Production Controller: Emily Noto